A HOME FOR ALL
SEASONS

A HOME FOR ALL SEASONS

Kristin Perers

Photography by James Merrell

RYLAND
PETERS
& SMALL

LONDON NEW YORK

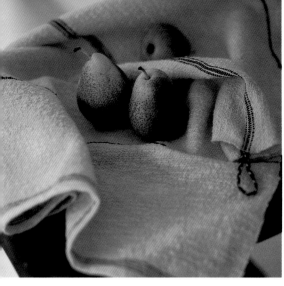

To my Mom and Dad, who gave me a childhood home so grounded in love that it gave me the freedom to fly

Designers **Mark Latter and Vicky Holmes**
Senior Editor **Sian Parkhouse**
Stylist **Kristin Perers**
Illustrator **Kristin Perers**
Creative Director **Jacqui Small**
Publishing Director **Anne Ryland**

First published in the United States in 1998
as *Seasonal Home*
This edition published in 2003
by Ryland Peters & Small
519 Broadway
5th Floor
New York NY 10012
www.rylandpeters.com
10 9 8 7 6 5 4 3 2

The publishers are grateful for permission to quote
extracts from the following books:
p.8 *The Prophet* by Kahlil Gibran, Borzoi Books/Alfred
A. Knopf, copyright © Kahlil Gibran 1923, 1951 (renewal
by Administrators C.T.A. of Kahlil Gibran Estate, and
Mary G. Gibran); pp. 12 and 14 *Shelter for the Spirit* by
Victoria Moran, HarperCollins Publishers copyright
© 1997 Victoria Moran

Contents

Inspirations

"Your house shall not be an anchor but a mast"

Kahlil Gibran

Each season brings a different mood. The temperature and the quality of the light change: we want to feel cool and easy in summer and warm and cozy in winter. The seasons have an inevitable rhythm, but this can be lost in our modern lives, especially in the city. We now have electricity that allows us to work all night. Heating and air conditioning serve as instant temperature controls. These modern conveniences have certainly added to our lives but we are in danger of losing something as well—if we are not careful we could lose the harmony and balance that nature provides. Nature has its own pace, it can't be rushed: part of its beauty is in the process of time unfolding. What are the seasons but a play of opposites? The freedom of summer is a reaction to the hibernation of winter. Both heat and cold have their places, and darkness and shadow make us appreciate lengthening days all the more. The

Everyday wonders

anticipation of the first strawberries is what heightens their sweetness. These sensations cannot be rushed. Let your home have visual prompts for the feelings that each season brings. Why is it in spring that we feel the need to throw open our windows and do a clean sweep of the house? It is a reaction to the months of being shut inside. In summer we relax and mentally, if not physically, we go on vacation. In the fall we tidy up the year and try to complete all the tasks that have not been finished, and winter is time to look inward at our thoughts. Change is the only constant: apply this to your life and your home and use it as a reminder to observe the everyday wonders around you. Our responses to our external environment are what make a house a living home. Sometimes those responses can be small personal gestures, sometimes they are bold single strokes that make a room come alive. Details that evoke the seasons change the spirit of a room, allowing you and your home to be connected to the natural rhythm of the earth.

create seasonal still lifes

It is on walks that a lot of my own inspiration comes. Be it through a city park, a woodland glade, or along the seashore, I take in the sights and sounds, smells and textures of each changing season. As I go, I collect charms to take home as a reminder of the natural world. These collections become a

revolving display in my home, to be savored and enjoyed for a while and then changed and replenished as the seasons do. Your home is a blank canvas. It's fun to create tabletop still lifes by combining your favorite finds: twigs from last weekend's country walk, a simple jug filled with sweet peas blooming in the yard. Extend your enjoyment of your outdoor experience.

five environmental factors that
influence our well being:

light

sound

aroma

color

touch

I'm a true believer in the power of beauty. It can inspire, heal, and awaken your senses. Others may trivialize the importance of a pretty flower display, but I know what it does to my heart. Beauty is the gift the world gives us. A scent can bring back memories so sharply and immediately that sometimes it hurts. Sunlight on your skin after a long winter can chase away any cares. Your surroundings hold tremendous power on your moods and emotions, so use that power for positive effect.

nature gives us the variety we crave

"Discovering sacred space
in the midst of the
ordinary and to realize
that the ordinary has been
extraordinary all along."

Victoria Moran

"Summer is disruptive—too much heat and too much activity. But in the fall there is order, in winter there is tradition, and in the spring there is growth. Spring is when I'm need by my rose bushes and the grass and the flowers. I renew my house and it renews me."

Toni, Shelter for the Spirit

let what's going on outside influence what's going on inside

The garden and the vegetable market are great sources of inspiration. Follow the colors that nature offers each season. Watch how changing a vase of flowers from summer daisies to autumnal hydrangeas can alter the mood of a room. This simple change will leave you wanting to put away the breezy linens of summer and throw a rich

bring the whole beach
home in just one pebble

paisley shawl over the sofa, and then move
the furniture closer to the fire. One change
leads to another. Think of the joy of bringing
home an armful of sunflowers and the first
strawberries of the season. Place these on
your kitchen table and there is no doubt
summer has arrived!

"The best
things
in life
are free."

Spring plays hide and seek with us—here one day and gone the next. We can't quite put away our winter woolens, but we are yearning for a change, a freshness, to mark the birth of the new year that is upon us. No other season is waited for with such hope and anticipation. The first warm days send us outside smiling again. The earth sends up a rush of growth, and the world is young again. What are the essential elements that evoke this season? Imagine the suprise of color from the first crocus blooms, the heavenly scent of lily of the valley, or the

spring

song of birds returning to the garden. The world is full of potential. It's a delicate time, a time of renewal, when nature gives birth. Find creative ways to bring this excitement indoors. Forcing bulbs is one of the easiest and most satisfying of springtime pleasures. Use your imagination when looking for containers—you'll find a whole host of ideas in ordinary things you already have around the house. An old metal bucket can be loaded with Paperwhites, inexpensive enamel mugs look charming in a row with a hyacinth blooming in each.

Cherry, quince, and apple blossoms can be brought indoors for forcing. Split the ends of woody stems and stand them in a warm room. Sow seeds in wooden trays and place them on a window-sill. The emerging buds are a reminder of the earth's renewal.

The textures of spring are soft and welcoming – think of the softness of pussy willow or the fluff of a newly hatched chick. Take a cue from this and surround yourself with soft cotton knits, beautifully worn and faded floral chintzes, innocent gingham checks: all these reflect the delicate world that is emerging outside. Introduce soft colors that reflect nature's palette, such as shades of lilac, dusty pink and green. A splash of yellow daffodils on your kitchen table can in one stroke banish all memories of winter. Traditionally, it is a time to do a clean sweep of the house,

shake off the dust, and freshen the home. Wash the windows to let the longer daylight shine in. Use natural cleaning materials such as white vinegar, baking soda, and borax to ensure a healthy home as well as a clean one. Scrub wooden surfaces with beeswax polish for a glowing patina and a wonderful lingering scent.

The air is charged with energy and optimism, and the change in weather urges us to come out of hibernation to start socializing again. Be inspired by the new season's produce coming onto the market. and plan a meal around the surprises of spring. The subtle flavor of new potatoes with fresh mint, the youngest peas and asparagus will not be repeated again in the year. Catch a dose of spring fever and let your home burst forward with the same vibrancy as the season outside.

As the days lengthen, the light gets stronger, the weather warmer, and summer is here. The elements make us feel like relaxing, mentally winding down. Summer is about freedom. Freedom from routine, freedom even from the constraints of clothes. Life takes on a more laidback approach. Summer decorating should reflect this and at its best be like going on vacation, easy and relaxing. Surrender to the season and simplify the home, giving yourself some breathing space. In summer the house becomes a shady

summer

retreat from the scorching weather outside. It's time to lighten the house, open windows, pare down bedding to a minimum. Roll rugs away and let bare feet run across cool floorboards. Change your drapes to a sheer white linen. Improvise and use a straw beach mat as a table runner or make a centerpiece of a bowl filled with sea glass found on a walk. A single starfish looks enchanting on a windowsill silhouetted against a brilliant blue sky. Fling a crocheted shawl over a table and place a vase on top overflowing with cow parsley. Summer is gone in a flash, so grab it while you can.

Be free-spirited with your home and let it be as spontaneous as the season. Move your furniture outside and make areas for enjoying the delights of the season. A day bed on the porch enveloped in mosquito netting or a huge hammock strung between two shady trees are all you need to entice you into a lazy day's reading.

Summer starts delicately and builds bolder as the season progresses. Outside colors become more intense to stand up to the stronger sunlight. Take a cue from the fuchsia cosmos growing in your garden and add stronger accents indoors. Let it be as simple as a bowl of nectarines or a pot of marigolds. Flowers are in abundance at this time of year, so don't hold back. Make full clusters of flowers arranged in a casual way as they would naturally grow in the garden. Herbs needn't be reserved for the kitchen and cooking. Mix mint, rosemary, and

sage in with your flowers arrangements or grow them in a bedroom windowbox. The scent through an open window at night will assure sweet dreams.

Cooking becomes an outdoor activity inspired by southern climates. From croissants on the porch to clambakes in the evening, we want to spend every waking minute outside. Even if you are stuck in the city for the summer, you can transport yourself temporarily by cooking a meal inspired by the destination of your choice. With the availability of ingredients and produce from all over the world today, it is easy to bring home the tastes, scents, and colors of almost any exotic land. Creating a romantic atmosphere for dining al fresco can be as easy as throwing a few pillows and a tablecloth outside and filling jars with sand and lighting candles in them. All you need is a few shooting stars to finish off the night.

Beachcombing

To look closely at a handful of sea glass is to look at the sea. Sea glass has all the elements of the sea: the color, frosty texture, and worn saltlike transparency all convey the combination of sea, sand, and light. One piece alone shimmers like sunlight on water, and in combination the various colors bounce off each other like an entire seaside landscape. Gathering these little jewels on waterside walks is a natural enjoyment for children and adults alike. A handful brought home can serve as a reminder of the sea in much the same way that a painting or photograph would. I love strolling along creating mini color palettes in my hand as I go. I'm always amazed at how nature sets out groups of colors that balance and play off each other perfectly. I add and edit as I walk, enjoying the way a palette can change with the addition of a single new color.

For a constant reminder of the summer all around me, I've introduced these palettes in my home. I've picked out paint colors inspired by the palettes the seashore has produced, and I've painted some old porch furniture in various shades of green and white. Using a watered-down latex paint, I applied layer upon layer of the colors and then roughly sanded back the paint to reveal all the different shades underneath, giving a sea-washed effect both in the colors and the textured finish.

left A mobile of sea glass, driftwood, and string reflects summer sun.
right Everything about sea glass— its color, texture, and the way it reflects light—is a reminder of the seaside.
top far right The color of sea glass translated into paint: used in multiple thin layers on furniture, it will create a beautifully worn seaside effect.
below far right An old rocker, a trolley, and even a galvanized tub are painted in colors inspired by the glass. Grass reeds are a natural complement since they grow in the same environment.

The calendar turns and the sun-baked fields of summer become the harvest of autumn. Colors change from bright to burning. Autumn is the cumulation of the year, what nature has been striving for: abundance. The cooler weather sends us into a whirl of activity: crops are harvested, children return to school. There's a nip in the air as we kick up our heels to squeeze every drop out of life before winter's blanket sets in. Celebrations start, city life heats up again, and the social calendar will be full until the new year before you know it. At

autumn

the autumn equinox, day and night are equal, life seems to get back to routine. It's time to organize the home, get your storage sorted and prepare for the busy season ahead. The palette of fall is a sophisticated one: golden yellows blend into fiery reds, with a mix of orange in between and a crimson edge. It is this sort of palette in nature that makes the rich pattern of a paisley or the heather weave of a tweed seem so appropriate in the fall. Colors have depth—think of the faded flame-stitch pattern of a kilim rug or the umber stripes of an Indian serape.

Touches of these fabrics will help warm the home as the season gets colder. Just as you retrieve the warmer items from your closet, digging your walking boots and your waterproof jackets out of storage, so you should warm your house.

Pears are the perfect symbol of the season: everthing about them, from their rich colors to their full curvy shape, expresses the ripeness of the world at this time. First seen overflowing on a tree, then plucked and enjoyed as a still life in a bowl, only next to be baked and eaten in a pie. The wonder of nature has many moments. Pumpkins and squash, too, have a dual life. The insides are scooped out and made into hearty soups, while the shell can be used as a decorative container to serve the soup from, or Halloween lanterns filled with flickering candles.

Large wooden bowls filled with apples or nuts replace the floral decorations of summer. It is worth buying produce at a

farmer's market or an organic grocer since the fruit and vegetables retain the naturally occuring variety in size, shape, and color, instead of sterile uniformity. Sadly the supermarkets see such variations as imperfections instead of nature's wonder.

Find creative ways to bring nature inside. Look to what is left in the yard. Flowers such as rudbeckia, nigella, poppies, and sunflowers have wonderful sculptural seed heads, giving them a life long after what is normally considered their prime. Combine spiky thistles and plump rose hips with turning foliage for vibrant autumnal displays. Dry sage in the fireplace then use it to kindle the first autumnal fire—folklore has it this cleans the atmosphere, ridding your home of any negative spirits that could be lurking about. Acorns and pine cones are to autumn what pebbles and shells are to summer. Collected on woodland walks, they can dot the house with rustic charm.

Autumn fruits

Color plays a vital role in influencing our moods and emotions. Yellow is the color of the sun, energizing and happy; red the color of passion; blue evokes the seaside. With all the specialized paints available today, I feel like a kid in a candy store, but a good rule is to decorate to reflect nature's pallete—nature usually gets it right. Indigenous plants and landscapes will often hold the key to which colors will work best indoors.

Try color accents such as painting the ceiling sky blue, a Georgian tradition. If you are not bold enough to paint a whole room why not just one wall? Even the inside of a cupboard painted in a contrasting color can make you smile each time you open it. Or my solution to sudden color fetishes is to paint my current favorite onto a large canvas. You can buy prestretched canvas in smaller sizes or make your own using stretchers from any artists' supply store, a few yards of canvas, and a staple gun. Don't feel intimidated because you are painting on canvas. Apply the paint in the same way you would color-wash a wall, in thin watered-down layers. When you tire of one color simply paint it over with your new favorite.

left Seasonal fruits provide the inspiration for an autumnal color story. **right** A large canvas is painted in tonal shades of grape, working as a backdrop to the jewel shades of the rich velvet and silk pillow covers and throw, bringing warmth to an otherwise monochrome room.

Winter comes upon us, and the world is at rest again. Days are short and the weather can be dreary. We fight the elements in winter more than any other time of year. But a northern gale and gray skies make us appreciate all the more the comforts of home. Winter is the time when nature hibernates, and we are not excluded. To protect yourself from harsh weather, make a cozy nest for yourself and curl up in front of a crackling fire with warm woolen blankets. Drink hot chocolate and listen to soothing music while the snow falls peacefully outside. Take

winter

long candlelit baths scented with aromatic oils. Mull hot cider, infusing the room with the smell of apples and cinnamon. Activity moves indoors, and this is the perfect time of year to get ahead with projects and crafts. Make room for these activities by designating a table as a hobby table where materials can be kept out. Or start a project basket and keep it on hand. A sweater you are knitting not only has a better chance of being finished, but also looks lovely if it is lying in a basket waiting to be picked up. If your creative endeavors are allowed to sit comfortably within a home, they add to the life and spirit of a place.

When days are short, compensate for the all-pervasive darkness by introducing cheerful colors and uplifting patterns in your home. The Scandinavians, who have one of the harshest of winter climates, do this so well: think of their bright checks and traditional knitting patterns. Scottish tartans have the same effect—warming but upbeat. Pamper yourself by surrounding yourself with tactile textures. A lot of the effort put into a home in winter has to do with chasing both the cold and the blues away. Bring out fabrics with a luxurious touch, such as velvet, corduroy, moleskin, and angora. Wrap yourself in one of the wonderful fake furs throws that are available now (or could be easily made).

In winter the earth reveals its skeleton. Think of the wonderful sculptural form of the witchhazel tree, how magnificent a single branch looks when brought indoors. Clipped box and bay laurel

stand alone in the garden, their neat ordered shapes a somehow welcome rest for the eye after the blazing autumnal palette. Wreaths can be made from what's left in the garden, the circle signifying the completion of the year. Try making one out of twigs if no greenery is available—the barren simplicity in a room can be its own sort of poetry.

Flowers are scarce, so turn to fruit and foliage for freshening a room. Eucalyptus is said to have medicinal qualities and will last a long time: its elegance remains even when it is dried. Bowls of oranges and lemons can add a bright spark of color to a room. Become an indoor gardener in winter and use this time to dream and plan your summer garden or windowboxes. Mark the new year by planting an amaryllis on January 1 and enjoy its beauty at every stage as it unfolds along with the new year.

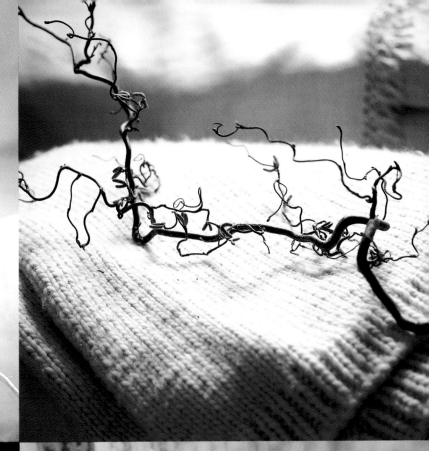

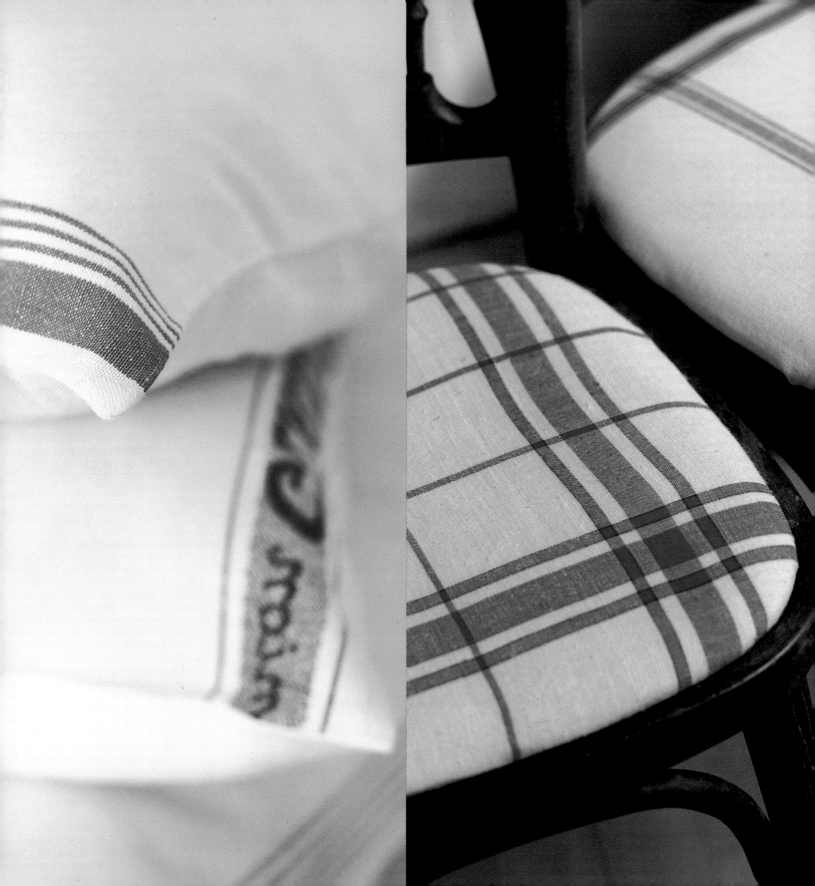

Creations

Display

A HOME SHOULD REVEAL THE PERSONALITIES OF ITS INHABITANTS. AT ITS BEST IT SHOULD BE A PORTRAIT OF WHO YOU ARE. IT IS THE SMALL TOUCHES, THE VIGNETTES WE CREATE WITH THE OBJECTS THAT HOLD MEANING TO US, THAT WILL GIVE A HOME ITS UNIQUE CHARACTER. IT IS THESE SMALL DETAILS THAT TRANSFORM A HOME INTO A PERSONAL SPACE. LOOK AT YOUR HOUSE AS AN ARTIST WOULD AND HAVE FUN CREATING VIGNETTES AS A PAINTER WOULD A STILL LIFE. Be spontaneous and use the seasons and changing light and temperature to act as prompters to reconsider the things around you. Let what's going on outside influence what happens inside your home. Rotate your favorite things from room to room to keep your home alive and in motion. Use what you already have in a different context, and you'll be surprised how stimulating your things will look when literally seen in a new light. I love scavenging mementos from nature to use within my home in fleeting still lifes. It is a way of holding onto memories of a time and place. Create tension by mixing hard and soft objects, and by placing large shapes next to small. Mix the past with the present. Punctuate something by displaying it en masse. Keep your displays revolving, and in turn your home will feel very much alive. These are the touches that will fill your house with soul and make those living with in it blossom. Creativity is something we all have and it needn't be shown through the customary avenues of painting or writing; it can be as simple as the way we arrange flowers or objects on our mantel. Our surroundings hold tremendous power over our moods and emotions—use that power to positive effect.

Personal mementos

It needn't be serious artwork to hang on the wall—a collection of favorite mementos such as postcards, children's drawings, and sketches can give your home a more personal feel. Embrace the possibilities that change has to offer and create transient displays reflecting your mood and interests at the moment. Visuals will remain more spontaneous and stimulating if they are fashioned in a manner that allows for this continual influx of new ideas.

left A laundry line strung across the wall is a great
way to hang an ever-changing array of watercolors.
above Postcards and photographs reflect the mood of a summer
vacation. **top right** Victorian seaweed prints are pinned casually to the wall,
balancing the formality of the framed picture. **center right** Polaroids and lichen
make an intimate winter's display. **bottom right** A screen with clips nailed onto it is
the venue for a changeable show of postcards and pictures.

1 Start with three layers of materials. Cut the foamcore board and the batting to fit your frame. Cut the ticking 4 inches (10 cm) wider all around than the foamcore.

You will need

empty frame
foamcore board
synthetic batting
cotton ticking
ribbon
package tape
map pins

2 Wrap the ticking tautly around the foamcore, sandwiching the batting between them. Tuck the corners in neatly to form a miter, trimming the excess fabric first. Secure the ticking with small pieces of tape.

Notice board

At last—a stylish bulletin board that will look as good in your living room as in a home office. The frame, found in a thrift shop, is made out of old pine molding. It's been painted with layers of latex in varying shades of white for a mellowed look. Old family photos and personal mementos can be tucked throughout the ribbons without damage from pins and layered and changed as new favorites arrive.

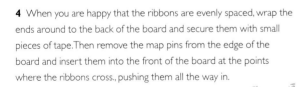

3 To attach the ribbon in a diagonal pattern, work from the front of the board. Secure the pieces at each end on the edge of the board with map pins, pulling them taut and allowing enough ribbon to overlap to the back of the board.

4 When you are happy that the ribbons are evenly spaced, wrap the ends around to the back of the board and secure them with small pieces of tape. Then remove the map pins from the edge of the board and insert them into the front of the board at the points where the ribbons cross., pushing them all the way in.

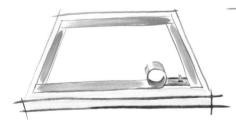

5 Push the completed board into the frame, and finish it with package tape, making sure you seal the raw edges of the ticking and the ribbon.

Transitory displays

Hanging paintings on unyielding walls can be an intimidating project. You have to be sure that you are not going to change your mind too soon, because once you have banged nails into the walls, changing their position can be difficult. To answer this problem, I've devised a display wall in my home using narrow shelves 3 inches (8 cm) wide. Here I prop an ever-changing variety of sketches and photos. By the same principle, you could hang a single big painting above your mantelpiece and then layer smaller pieces in front of it by simply leaning them against the others. This allows you freedom to add an inspiring postcard or a new photo to the display when the mood strikes.

left It doesn't have to be art for you to hang it on the walls. If you cannot afford original artworks, your walls don't have to go bare. Try hanging quilts, clothing, or textiles, or even a collection of hats, as here. Garden chairs or a flower-pot borrowed from the yard add to the breezy summery feel suggested by a collection of straw hats. **right** Alcove shelving continued across a chimney makes a perch for an ever-changing exhibition.

Make the everyday beautiful

You don't need to surround yourself with a host of material possessions in order to create a beautiful home—instead, make the everyday beautiful. By giving thought to the objects we hold and use in our daily rituals, you can make these mundane routines more pleasurable. There is an appealing honesty to hand-crafted objects that are designed with simplicity and function in mind. Another bonus is they don't beg to be hidden away when not in use. A vintage watering can or tin dust-pan and wooden-handled brush will not scream out at you in a room like modern plastic versions would. Often, too, these things don't cost any more than their mass-produced equivalents would. Look around you at the objects you use constantly: kitchen utensils, pots and pans, coat hangers, even scrubbing brushes. With some thought, all these things can be a pleasure to the hand as well as the eye.

above The serene rhythm of empty hangers provides a moment's pause. **right** When art materials and tools are this beautiful, they don't need to be hidden away out of sight.

Remember how as a child in school you would take in contributions to the class nature table? Recreate this idea in your home to add vitality and energy to a room. As it is usually the focal point in a room,

a home is not a static place

a mantelshelf is the perfect place to display an array of finds that change as often as the weather does: a row of pine cones graduating in size; a pile of pebbles from a coastal walk grouped according to color; a plain white pitcher filled with Queen Anne's lace.

Display can be a form of visual poetry. **above, left to right** A sketch taped casually on the wall allows for easy and frequent changes. Straw textures accentuate a summery mood. Rocks from a summer vacation are sorted and labeled, holding memories of a time and place in a jar. **below, left to right** Stones collected on the beach are gilded with hearts. A single apple plucked from an orchard on a weekend walk is as beautiful as any object of art. Twigs from the same walk create a natural sculpture that can be enjoyed and then changed as the seasons evolve. **right** A large cloud painting on an unframed artist's canvas simply pinned onto the wall serves as a perennial backdrop for a layering of seasonal mantel displays.

Painted cupboard

Thrift shops are great places to scout inexpensive furniture. Look for pieces with good proportions and clean simple lines. Many of the things for sale can easily be transformed with this simple paint technique. The technique uses water-based paint so it is easy to do with a minumum of fuss and no chemicals. A broad flat space is the perfect place to put a favorite motif, such as the dove I've painted here.

1 To prepare the cupboard, lightly sand it, then wipe it with a damp rag. Using the middle-tone paint, apply a first coat over the entire surface. When it has dried you can apply thinner layers of paint. Mix the darkest shade with 3 parts paint to 1 part water then apply it thinly to the panel sections of the cupboard, brushing in the direction of the wood grain. Dilute the palest paint the same way and apply it to the frame surrounding the panels. Let it dry.

2 Dilute the middle-toned paint and apply it over the entire cupboard again. Repeat this layering process 3 times, allowing each coat to dry before applying the next. Finish with the separate coats of dark and light paints. Roughly sand the cabinet, working in the direction of the wood grain. As you sand you will reveal the different layers of paint to create a soft graduated tonal effect. At this stage, you can if you wish apply more layers or even a final coat of very thin paint that has been diluted 1 part paint to 1 part water.

3 Enlarge the template of the dove to your required size and use a pencil to trace it onto the cupboard door.

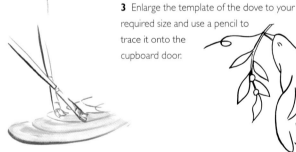

4 Using the artist's brush and the lightest color, paint in the body of the bird. Apply the paint in short strokes, twisting the brush at the end to create the effect of feathers. Using longer strokes paint the tail and wings, following the direction of the feathers. On the wings, paint the longer underfeathers first and then the shorter top ones over the top. The paint may dry out and become slightly powdery, but this will help to create a raised, three-dimensional image.

5 When the dove is dry, apply two coats of acrylic varnish to the entire cupboard to seal the surface.

Watch as the year blossoms

Flowers and foliage add life to a room. I used to spend a fortune on fresh cut flowers, but now I've realized that with a bit of ingenuity I can make my own arrangements from what is available in my small yard. I like to use indigenous flowers and foliage rather than exotic imports as this secures a sense of place, and seasonal blooms help to ground you in the revolution of the year. In spring, I become an indoor gardener, indulging myself with the delight of forcing bulbs. A tub of Paperwhites can usher in spring long before the weather does. In the fall I turn to berries, rosehips, and seasonal foliage. Small posies can have as much impact as larger displays with some thought to their placement. Think of the places you go to during your daily routine, such as your bathroom sink. A small posy here will cheer you when you wake up in the morning and again before you go to bed at night.

Floral displays don't have to be overstuffed vases. A small simple gesture is often enough to act as a reminder of what is happening outdoors. Single flowers look great in milk bottles or bigger bouquets in kitchen storage jars. Don't be afraid to place humble containers such as these on your most elegant dining table—it's the mix that makes it fun.

Flower mirror

Mirrors provide wonderful opportunities for small decorative gestures because our daily routine means that we look into them at least once a day. Pressing small hydrangea flower heads between glass preserves their fragile beauty, carrying the feel of summer throughout the year. The colors will fade gradually, but this will merely add to their muted charm. A backless frame holding two sheets of glass (see *opposite page*) can act as a showcase for the seasons. Fill it with a natural succession of flowers and foliage, from the delicate fronds of verdant evergreen ferns in winter to vibrant orange nasturtium flowers in summer, spidery maple leaves in their jeweled fall colors and simple sweet violets in spring.

You will need

1 piece of picture frame glass cut to size
1 piece of mirror glass cut to size
fresh flowers for border
blotting paper
double-sided tape
heavy-duty linen tape
ribbon

1 Press individual fresh flower heads between sheets of blotting paper. Place them in a large book and stack other heavy books on top. Leave them for at least 3 weeks to dry out completely.

2 Have a piece of picture frame glass and a piece of mirror glass cut to size. Ask your glazier to make 2 holes at the top of each piece, 1 ½ inches (3.5 cm) from the top edge and 2 inches (5cm) apart.

3 Cut small pieces of double-sided tape and stick them to the back of each flower. Lay the mirror flat and stick the fowers evenly around the edge.

4 Carefully lay the glass on top of the mirror to seal in the flowers and then tape each corner diagonally using the heavy-duty tape to secure the glass.

5 To hang the mirror, thread the ribbon through the 2 holes and tie it in a bow.

Soft furnishings

I HAVE A PASSION FOR TEXTILES. TO ME, CHANGING FABRICS IS ONE OF THE EASIEST WAYS TO REINVENT A ROOM. A BED, CHAIR, TABLE, OR SOFA CAN AND SHOULD CHANGE FROM WINTER TO SUMMER. BY CHANGING SLIPCOVERS, CURTAINS, TABLE CLOTHS, BED LINENS, PILLOW COVERS, OR JUST THROWING A PIECE OF FABRIC OVER A SIDETABLE, YOU CAN IN ONE STROKE CHANGE THE ATMOSPHERE OF A ROOM. Think of it as creating wardrobes for your home! Slipcovers can be a bold way to achieve a quick changeover. Even a couple of side chairs in different guises can punctuate the seasonal mood of a room. Or transform your sofa with a paisley shawl and change of pillow covers. I have a small collection of throws I use just for this purpose. Ever useful, a throw can reinvent itself as a tablecloth, a bed throw, or even an ad hoc drape. Throws add instant texture and are a way to add color or pattern to a room without making a long-term or expensive commitment. Make seasonal nests for yourself: in winter throw a fake fur blanket in front of the fire and snuggle up with a cup of hot chocolate. A summer hammock can be strewn with pillows made from vintage prints for extra comfort. The wonderful thing about fabrics is they need not be permanent; you can be a bit more adventurous with pattern and color as they can be revolved so easily around the house and throughout the year. Layer and unlayer as the weather dictates.

Summer shirting

Don't limit yourself to furnishing fabrics when you are looking for ideas for your home. Fashion fabrics used out of context can often be much less expensive and add a certain whimsy to a room. Here, inspiration for a number of decorating ideas is found in a classic man's formal striped shirt. It adds the same crisp clean freshness to a room that it does to a wardrobe.

Buy a few yards in a combination of coordinating stripes and have fun making pillow cases, laundry bags, even duvet covers. Quilting is an excellent way of using up fabric scraps and today with machine sewing it needn't be the tedious labor-intensive chore it once was. Trimmings such as ribbons and buttons can be found in abundance at antique markets.

Second-hand clothing can be a springboard for inspiration. Men's nightshirts from the early part of the century often have beautiful mellowed stripes, and women's dirndl skirts from the 1950s can have amusing, slightly kitsch, conversational prints that work well on flat surfaces such as roller shades or pillows covers, so that you can appreciate the large-scale design. Worn-out denims and canvas can be cut into patches and stitched together to cover a footrest; the fabric will still be sturdy enough to take lots of wear and tear.

Look to your closet for the things you don't wear any more. Maybe the style or size doesn't suit any more, but you have been hanging on to it because you still like the fabric. There's a whole treasure of goodies tucked away in your wardrobe.

right Summer shirting sparks off an array of decorating ideas in the bedroom—from the patchwork quilt displayed on the wall to the checked pillow sham. The duvet is made from sections of shirting pieced together. **far right** Spacious drawstring laundry and storage bags are made from shirt fabric trimmed with contrasting grosgrain ribbon.

Autumnal Throw

Patchwork is one of the thriftiest ways of using up fabric scraps. It's a technique our grandmothers used and for good reason. This fireside throw is made of odd pieces of wool tweed combined with a luxurious velvet trim and lambswool backing. It is sturdy enough to be thrown on the floor yet welcoming enough to snuggle into.

You will need

assorted pieces of tweed to cut into scraps

lambswool for backing

velvet

thread

1 Cut squares from the tweed fabrics. The ideal size is about 4 inches (10 cm) square. Sew 10 squares together to form a long strip. Make another 12 strips in the same way so you have 13 in all, and then sew the strips together. Press the seams open flat.

2 For the border, cut 2 pieces of velvet 8 inches (20 cm) wide and 8 inches longer than the tweed panel, and 2 pieces 8 inches wider than the panel and 8 inches long. Right sides facing, join one short piece to one long piece. Make a triangle by folding the corners in. Sew along this line, trim the excess fabric and press the seams open. Join all 4 pieces in this way to make the border.

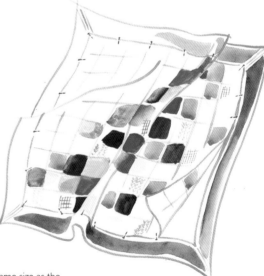

3 With the border wrong side out, pin the tweed panel to one side of the border, right sides together and pin, baste, and sew around all 4 sides.

4 Cut the backing the same size as the tweed panel and pin it to the back opening, right sides together. Sew around 3 sides, leaving the other side open. Press the seams open and turn the throw right side out through the open side. Slipstitch the opening closed and each corner of the back panel at the inside edge to secure.

Using everyday objects

You do not have to spend a fortune decorating your home with purchased soft furnishings—basic household items can be an endless source of inspiration. To me, one of the simple pleasures of life is the humble dishtowel. Its clean fresh checks and stripes makes me think of spring all year long. Collect different ones and sew them into various shapes and guises: they can be transformed into curtains, a patchwork for a tablecloth, be turned into pillow covers, or simply hung for use on a wall. New ones look fresh and bright, but old ones have their own faded charm too. Try scouting antique markets. Old French linen dishtowels are especially beautiful.

far left Nothing could be simpler than using heavy cotton dishtowels to cover the seat pads of wooden chairs. **left** A variety of old and new dishtowels make for refreshing cushion covers. **above** A soft Roman shade made from a blue-and-white checked dishtowel print lends a spring feel all year. **far right top** Necessity makes for clean living: hung in a row these towels make a practical and pretty display. **far right bottom** Half a vintage tablecloth makes a café curtain.

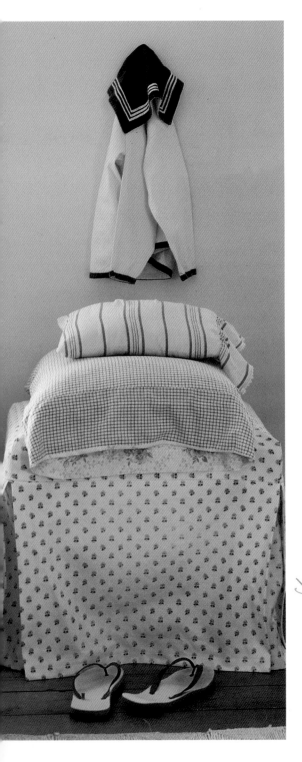

Middy pillow

You will need

an adult-size sailor top—look in antique markets and secondhand stores

thread

I love vintage clothing and I incorporate pieces into my home as display. Often you find garments that are damaged and so sold cheaply. But that needn't hinder you: with careful cutting you can salvage the good bits and make up small accessories.

1 Cut three pieces from the sailor top. Cut a rectangular section from the collar, and cut one piece from the back and a longer piece from the front, as indicated in the diagram. Cut each piece 1 inch (2.5 cm) wider than the collar to allow for the seams. The back piece should be equal in length to the collar and the front piece. Add 1 inch seam allowance to the length on the back and front pieces. Remove the sleeve patch, the pocket, and the necktie from the top and retain them.

2 On the front piece, turn in a double hem along one of the short sides onto the right side. Attach the collar to the front piece by stitching along the top of the hemmed edge, keeping the hemmed edge visible.

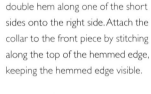

3 Sew the patch to the pocket and then sew the pocket onto the center of the front of the pillow. Make 2 buttonholes on the collar section, ½ inch (1 cm) apart and wide enough for the necktie.

4 With right sides together, sew the back and front pieces along three sides, but do not sew the collar. Turn right side out then topstitch the collar in place.

5 Thread the necktie through the buttonholes and tie it in a bow. To secure it, slipstitch it in place with a few stitches at the back of the buttonhole.

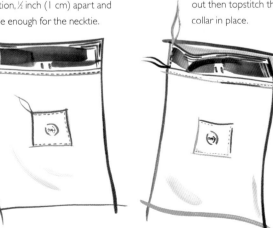

Button lampshade

Here's an idea for buying something ready made and then personalizing it. After looking for lampshades for my home I became discouraged, mainly by the outrageous prices. So I turned to the local department store and bought the simplest, most inexpensive shades I could find, then sat myself down for an hour in the sun and used ribbons and vintage buttons to create something a bit more special. And when you haven't spent a huge amount of money you will be inclined to change your lampshades more frequently!

You will need

a plain purchased lampshade

ribbon for trim

approximately 10 pearl buttons

all-purpose glue

double-sided tape

1 To work out how much ribbon you need, wrap it around the top and bottom of the lampshade, adding ½ inch (1 cm) for the overlap. Lay the ribbon flat and spread an even amount of glue onto the back of the ribbon. Carefully stick the ribbon to the lampshade, lining up the overlap with the seam of the lampshade and tucking under the raw edges.

2 Stick small pieces of double-sided tape on the back of the buttons and place them on the lampshade, adjusting them as necessary. When you are happy with the arrangement, mark the position of each button with a pencil, remove the tape from the buttons, and glue them firmly in place.

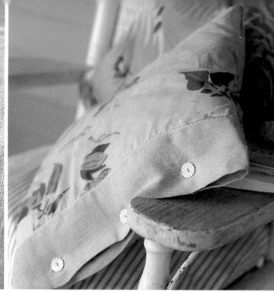

Use cushion covers as accessories: change them to suit your mood and the atmosphere you want to create. Make them out of fabric remnants or try sales for bolt ends sold cheaply. Use bandanas or tie a scarf around a throw pillow for a quick fix. I have one big wicker chair that I call my seasonal chair. I change the seat cushion by tucking different fabrics around it and switch scatter cushions every once in a while. It is the first thing I see when I walk into my living room, and it's always a welcoming note.

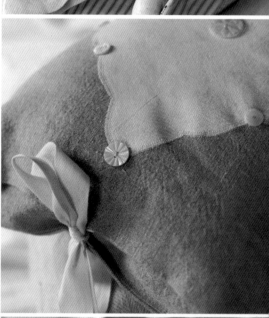

Decorating cushions

Daisy tablecloth

Even the most unsightly table can be transformed with the throw of a cloth. Here, my husband's old workbench reinvents itself as a sideboard. I don't like spending hours of time on these projects so I used a machine zig-zag stitch for the appliqué and saved hours of labor.

You will need

medium weight artist's canvas (you can find this at most good art supply stores)

similar-weight white linen

pencil

thread

4 large buttons (I've used antique ones)

1 Wash the artist's canvas to preshrink it; let it dry. It has a tendency to crack and have a rumpled look after washing, which adds to the character of the fabric. Measure the table you wish to cover and cut pieces for the top and back, allowing 1 inch (2.5 cm) all around each piece for seam allowance. The front and side panels should ideally be cut from one long piece of fabric, and you should allow an extra 8 inches (20 cm) added to the seam allowance

for each of the two box pleats at the front corners. If you need to join lengths of canvas to make the front and side piece, position the seams so they will be hidden in the corner pleats.

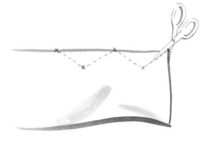

2 Prewash the linen. Measure the bottom edge of the front and side pieces and cut a piece of linen to this length and 12 inches (30 cm) deep. Again, if you need to join lengths, hide the seams in the box pleat. To make the border, mark equal distances along the the top edge for the peaks, then mark the distance halfway between each of these marks 4 inches (10 cm) below the first row of marks for the valleys. Cut from dot to dot to form the zigzag.

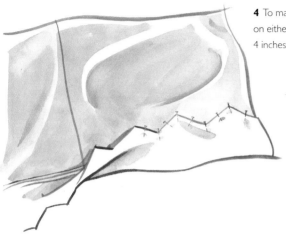

4 To make the corner pleats fold in 2 inches (5 cm) on either side, so that the total width of the pleat is 4 inches (10 cm). Pin the pleat in place and make sure

3 Sew the border to the bottom of the front and sides section of the table cloth, with the right side of the border facing the wrong side of the cloth. Then flip the border over to hide the seam and pin it in place. Sew along the edge of the zigzags using a very narrow zigzag stitch to attach the border to the cloth, and then press.

the center lines up with one corner of the table. Make a second pleat for the other front corner, adjusting the first pleat if necessary. Press the pleats, then sew them in place ½ inch (1 cm) below the upper edge.

5 Cut petal shapes from white linen and pin them in place on the front of the cloth, and then sew them using a small zigzag stitch. Sew a button to the center of each flower. To assemble the tablecloth, hem the bottom long edge of the back panel, and then sew the pieces together as shown in step 1. Press open the seams, clip the corners, and turn right side out.

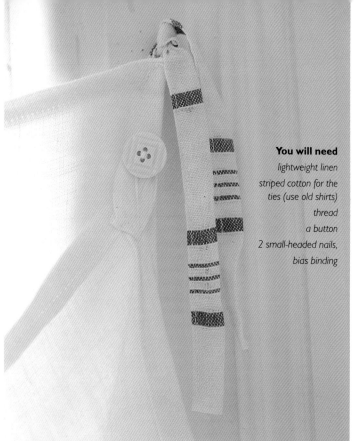

You will need

*lightweight linen
striped cotton for the
ties (use old shirts)
thread
a button
2 small-headed nails,
bias binding*

Summer curtain

Sheer white café curtains are a great way to add privacy without blocking a view or the light. Here is proof that so often the simplest ideas are the best. Take short cuts with sewing where you can—for instance, if the fabric has an attractive selvage, incorporate it into the design it and save yourself time hemming.

1 Measure the area of the window you want to cover and take the dimensions of the curtain from that, adding 1 inch (2.5 cm) all around for the hems. Cut the linen and turn under a double hem on all 4 sides.

2 For the ties, cut 2 pieces of cotton 16 inches (40 cm) long by 1¾ inches (4.5 cm) wide. Press under ½ inch (1 cm) all around, press in half lengthwise, and sew around 3 sides.

3 Sew the ties to the top corners of the curtain, placing them diagonally across the corners.

4 Make a loop from bias binding and sew it onto the wrong side of the lower left corner of the curtain.

5 Sew a button 1½ inches (3.5 cm) below the right tie. To hang the curtain, hammer a nail on each side of the window frame and knot the ties on the nails. To fold back the curtain, hang the loop on the button.

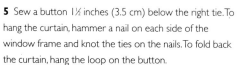

Living spaces

Relaxing

THE LIVING ROOM IS USUALLY THE FIRST ROOM YOU SEE WHEN YOU WALK INTO A HOUSE—IT IS THE ROOM THAT WELCOMES YOU HOME. BUT IT IS A PUBLIC ROOM AS WELL AS A PRIVATE ONE, AND SO IT IS VERY EASY TO SLIP INTO THE TRADITION OF MAKING THIS ROOM THE MOST FORMAL IN A HOUSE. PERSONAL TOUCHES ARE OFTEN RESERVED FOR OTHER ROOMS SUCH AS BEDROOMS. But this can lend a stiff welcome. A house should reveal its inhabitants slowly, drawing a visitor in. A living room that is inviting and lived in can bring a warm welcome to you and guests each time they come through the door, making you and them feel much more at home. Try breaking down the space between private and public, mixing formal pieces with more informal whimsical touches that make a house a home. Simple ideas can have a big impact, and rooms that change with the calendar year make a house that houses your soul and not just your body. I learned a good lesson recently: I realized that the room in my house I felt most at home in was my top-floor studio. It is filled with sketches and photos casually pinned up on the wall, and an array of objects of personal meaning and inspiration that is constantly changing. In contrast, I would keep my living room clean and more guarded. I wasn't living in it, but saving it for special occasions, and I found when I brought people into the room it didn't say anything about me. Then I thought, why not treat this room as an extension of myself, as my studio naturally is? Why not make my living space as alive as I do my designated creative environment? A living room should be just that: a room to live in.

The mood of a room will change as the seasons do. I think the first view one sees when walking into a room is the most important and that means giving the room a focal point. If you are lucky enough to have a big fireplace, this will inevitably become the focus in winter. Even if it is not a working one, it can be filled with candles to create the illusion of firelight. In the summer daylight becomes more important, so the windows naturally receive more attention. Replace your heavy winter curtains with a more lightweight sheer fabric and move the furniture around so that the window is easily accessible for opening and closing, allowing the summer sunshine to pour in.

A city loft with a soft touch celebrates the changing seasons. **left** An open-plan space is divided off with drapes that change from a rich dark brown to a sheer white cotton. A moveable screen is used to focus attention on the dining area, creating a more intimate space for a winter dinner party. **right** The drama of an overscaled branch of quince blossom ushers in the arrival of spring. **far right, from top** A patchwork of vintage dishtowels makes a refreshingly different tablecloth. The mantelpiece gives this small area a focus and serves as a useful display area. Stretching a fabric panel across a fireplace when it is not in use is an effective way of shifting emphasis from what is an empty space for part of the year.

above Think of cushion covers as accessories for the home; they are the perfect venue for using daring prints as they can be changed so easily. A fake leopard print adds a dramatic touch, accenting this chair in winter. **below** Tableware need not be matching. An eclectic mix of candles and glasses adds a personal touch. Elegant white roses complement the look beautifully.

This romantic love nest is a charming alternative to the standard couch and two chairs seating arrangement. It is made simply by hanging curtains on a rod that is suspended from the ceiling. A single-bed size mattress is placed on a plywood base and covered with fabric; this sets the stage for an endless combination of textures and materials. **left** Winter is the time when we seem to dress up the home. Dramatic velvet curtains and bed dressings in bottle green set a glamorous scene. Mirrors can be used to open up a space and reflect light back into the room. **right** In spring a softer mood is conjured up with drapes of the palest sky blue and light layers of white bed linens covering the daybed. The wrought iron table has been moved for the season to another setting and is replaced by a small folding garden table. **below** Flowers have a beauty at each stage in their lives, like these spring peonies whose falling petals only add to their charm.

Change is the only constant. Satisfy your senses and follow your instincts: when it is rainy and cold, our instincts tell us to stay indoors and create nests; when it is warm and sunny, we are itching to go outside or to open the windows and let the outside in. Bring in symbols of the season as temporary displays in your home. Then go beyond those

symbols and ask yourself how you respond emotionally to each season, how the light, weather, and colors of each season make you feel. Satisfy these needs through changes in your physical environment.

How you feel today probably isn't the same as how you felt last year or even last week. So alter your rooms with your moods.

A spacious soothing white room becomes a nocturnal play of light and shadow in winter. **above left** Piles of cushions are scattered in front of a roaring hearth, making an inviting seasonal nest. **above center** An exotic atmosphere is created in winter using Turkish and Afghanistan textiles to drape the large white sofa, accented by black velvet roses, the glow of candlelight, and the scent of incense. **above** A deep pile of traditional knits from a mix of cultures is kept close at hand, as much for aesthetic as for practical reasons.

Keep your house alive and in motion; introduce objects that reflect your newest interests. A row of postcards propped on the mantel against a more formal oil painting can vary seasonally. The painting will probably stay in its place, but with different accents it will add freshness to a room. Your friends will be delighted with the visual stimulus each time they come over. Gather objects around you that hold memories of places or people who have been in your life, or use things from other areas of the house. A row of enamel pitchers usually kept in the kitchen can make a nice surprise as a temporary display on a living room table. The idea is to use what you already have in different ways.

above left In summer the room is kept spare and open—light floods in through bare windows, allowing a large gardenia plant to flourish. The floor is cleared of rugs to reveal the clear honeylike tones of the floorboards. Draped in its summer dressings, the sofa is brought forward into the room to make the most of the natural light. **above** Variously textured white and ivory embroidered linen and heavily slubbed fringed cotton blankets and rugs work as warm weather throws and cushion covers.

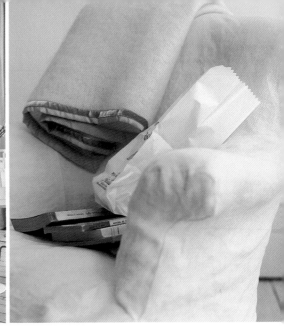

If you start with the main pieces of furniture, which in a living room will probably be seating, and then work toward the details, you will be able to put a room together that has a clean base with which you can then play to add seasonal details. The key is to have a versatile base that leaves room for possibilities.

The most important thing about living areas is to have comfort for your lifestyle. It is worth investing money in good comfortable seating, or the time into tracking these down in secondhand markets. These are the pieces that will form the skeleton of the room, so choose

above left Light, color, and space give this room a springtime feel. Colors inspired by the freshest buds continue the atmosphere. **above center** A chair gets a change of clothing when the mood strikes. Inexpensive straw shopping baskets work effectively as movable storage. **above right** A plain woolen blanket is personalized with velvet and silk ribbon. **below left** Flowers soften the edges of a room.

below center White floorboards and bare walls reflect light and emphasize the open space. Basic wooden trays planted with Paperwhites are all that is needed to add fragrance, color, and a flash of beauty. **below right** Plain white china plates look best on a simple trestle table painted primrose yellow. **right** Glass vases in varying sizes are treated like sculpture, making a rhythmic dance along the mantelpiece.

"If you have two loaves of bread
sell one and buy a hyacinth,
for it will feed your soul"

Persian poem

carefully. Nothing can beat a big, comfortable couch and chairs slipcovered in white or off-white fabric. Think of your lifestyle: perhaps the standard three-piece set isn't for you. Unconventional seating arrangements, such as a collection of odd armchairs or scattered floor cushions around a low table, could make you more comfortable. A daybed can be a romantic substitute for a sofa and it also serves as a guest bed when needed. This can be dressed and undressed as the seasons change. The key is to keep these investment pieces simple and classic, something you can live with for a long time, with seasonal adaptations such as throws and pillows layered on top.

Furniture should be easygoing in terms of care and up-keep—slipcovers should be made from prewashed fabric so they can be regularly thrown in the washing machine for easy cleaning. If you feel relaxed about your home, others will feel comfortable also.

After the seating is established, look at the table space. The coffee table has become a much-loved necessity in today's lifestyle, holding drinks and flowers, and serving as a central point around which to sit. Try placing a long bench in front of your couch to stack books and a tray of coffee on. It should be sturdy enough to withstand the odd pair of feet—nothing in your home should be so precious that you

can't kick off your shoes and rest your feet on top of it! Side tables can be picked up at flea markets; just look for great shapes that can be easily freshened up with a coat of paint. Or try stacking a pile of big art books on top of each other with a small tray on top—this can serve as a temporary side table, a convenient place to rest a glass. All these ad hoc ideas add a certain flexibility and give you the freedom to alter the movement of a room.

So often these days our rooms have to serve a multitude of purposes. My living room became a much friendlier place when I accepted the fact that a corner of it had to function as an office also.

far left A vacation home immediately says summer with a playful mix of pattern. **center left** Even a robust leather chair goes on vacation—strewn with floral pillows and a vintage tablecloth it is more comfortable for summer's bare legs. **center right** A flash of color comes from a glorious bunch of hibiscus floating in an enamel bowl. **below** Blur the definition between inside and out with doors flung wide open and the use of outside patio furniture and plants indoors.

Instead of hiding the fact I now celebrate it, and the feeling of industry this area generates, with notes and messages pinned on the wall, adds a wonderful life to this room. The function of our rooms changes from day to night as well as seasonally. Take note of this and make sure your furniture is as flexible as your lifestyle and use the room accordingly. Keep your furniture portable and move it as the seasons change, pulling it closer to the fire in winter and leaving things more open and spare in summer. Folding tables and chairs help to make a home more flexible. Try scouting out some of the wonderful old tables from the 1930s and '40s at flea markets or use old folding garden chairs for additional seating when needed. They can be easily shifted around to alter the function of a room as your needs change. In an open-plan space a screen is a great way to make an area more intimate and it can be moved around to disguise areas of clutter.

For flooring, my favorite treatment is always bare floorboards, whether they are painted, colorwashed to a pale pickled effect, or stained to bring out the natural effect of the wood. They require a minimum of upkeep, complement almost any decorating style, and they are versatile enough to adapt to differing climatic conditions. Large throw rugs can be used to add warmth in winter, and then rolled away or used as table throws in summer.

Making the transition from warm weather to cool, the subtle change in color and texture from white cotton sheeting to heavier natural unbleached linen slipcovers sets the stage for a changing season. **far left** Windows thrown open and a spray of delicate yellow tulips evoke sunshine. **left** The pleasure of color and texture stimulates the senses. **right** While the backdrop remains constant, the details of this room gently evolve from one season to the next: the collection of pillow covers becomes deeper in tone as the seasons progress, and the vase holds winter foliage.

above Signs of seasonal change are indicated by your wardrobe—when you put away your winter wrap and replace it with a lightweight raincoat to ward off spring showers, you know it is time to freshen your home also. **right and far right** Accents direct the focus from one season to the next, with the use of lighter colors for spring and deeper ones for the fall. All-season evergreen plants such as the sculptural clipped box look stylish potted in utilitarian galvanized buckets purchased from a local hardware shop. **far right top** Throws are the quickest way to warm a room and add a flash of seasonal color. **far right bottom** A dramatic over-scaled ceramic bowl generously filled with walnuts and placed directly on the floor creates a sense of abundance.

Playful vignettes incite curiosity
and invite the eye to wander.

Once the basics are established, accessories can be changed as your moods and needs require. Textiles are my primary way of adding seasonal interest. Cushions are comparable to jewelry: small details that lift an overall look. And as they take only a small amount of fabric, they are relatively inexpensive. You can use bolder fabrics and colors

above from left Antique ticking dresses a chair for winter. Ideas can be as impromptu as this drummer boy's jacket enlivened with a sprig from the garden. The last of the rose hips make an amusing still life. **below from left** The open-weave of this linen makes a charming slipcover. Look to unusual places for inspiration: this cover is actually a bath towel, but it is perfectly at home on a pillow. Enamel dishes hold a collection of seaside mementos. **right** Throw pillows in knitted wool covers create a cozy winter nest.

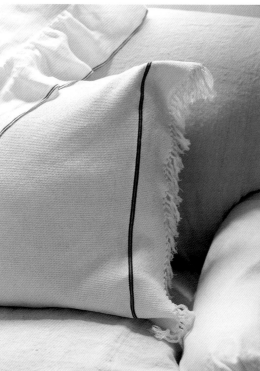

without fear, for when you tire of them they can be switched around and easily stored away until the next time. You can get away with using less-than-perfect remnants that are sold at a more reasonable price and just cut the fabric to hide any flaws. I also love collecting old textiles from markets and fashioning them into pillow covers.

Mixing and matching patterns can be fun. A standard ticking stripe looks fresh in spring layered next to a faded floral pillow, but it can work just as well in cold weather mixed with a rich paisley design. Throws are another way to instantly alter the mood of a room; I have a stack of blankets and bedcovers I keep just for this purpose. Don't forget to look in your closet for inspiration also. My velvet evening wrap lives on a big comfortable chair in the winter months, and in the summer a pretty crocheted shawl comes out of my closet to grace an ottoman. Try tucking a few yards of fabric around a seat cushion—

use tweed for color and warmth in the winter or try a gingham tablecloth in the same way for spring. A leather armchair can be covered with a voluminous old linen sheet to lighten the look for summer—don't worry about making a perfect set of fitted slipcovers, just knot the corners at the side. Or cover a small wooden chair in a succession of different fabrics so it becomes an accent in a room, complementing the seasons.

far left As the days slowly become chillier and light levels fall in autumn, gradually introduce warmer fabrics. Pillows covered in cashmere have the same comforting appeal as an old cardigan. **center left** The myriad colors offered by the autumnal palette of turning leaves are always an inspiration. **center right** Throws like this deeply fringed chocolate shawl are both a stylish and versatile way to add warmth and color to a room. The softly quilted cream cotton slipcovers on the sofa and ottoman are a perfect base for changing layers of seasonal dressing. **right** A generously proportioned bowl filled with windfall apples is both inviting and tempting.

Collections of textiles that are recycled for seasonal change in this way don't have to be put into hibernation and hidden away when they are not in use. Folded into neat piles and tied up with linen tape or brightly colored ribbon,
they can make satisfying
bundles that are attractive

Make space to contemplate the beauty of nature

enough to be displayed on book shelves or stacked in a corner against the wall. Or pack them in wicker baskets that can also serve as side tables. This way they can be enjoyed all year round as part of the decoration of your home, and they are a visible reminder to you to maintain a constant injection of new textures and colors to prevent the room from becoming static and dull.

far left An enclosed porch is perfectly balanced between indoors and out. **above from left** Take advantage of glorious views by positioning furniture to invite peaceful contemplation. Enjoy seasonal wonders outdoors, then bring individual finds home. **below from left** A stove extends the use of this room into winter. Savor still lifes such as the wonderful colors of herbal tea or a pile of logs.

Gathering and entertaining

SO MANY OF OUR TRADITIONAL YEARLY CELEBRATIONS REVOLVE AROUND THE PREPARATION OF FOOD. THESE FESTIVALS PLAY AN IMPORTANT ROLE IN MARKING THE CALENDAR YEAR AND HIGHLIGHTING THE DIFFERENT QUALITIES EACH SEASON BRINGS. THEY ADD A CERTAIN STRUCTURE TO OUR LIVES, KEEPING US IN TUNE WITH THE RHYTHMS OF NATURE. Although our supermarket shelves carry produce that has been flown in from other climates all over the globe, the cycles of scarcity and then abundance of fresh produce as it comes into its true season is still exciting. The first taste of fresh strawberries heralds the summer sun to come, and piles of jewellike tangerines, lemons, and limes cheer the winter months. The dining area is where you open your home to your friends, to the people you care to share your life with. It is a place for meeting and for conversation. A table should be conducive not just to beauty but to a discourse of ideas. Food, the way it is served, and the atmosphere in which it is served, is all part of this hospitality. It's a way of giving and allowing people to come into your life. The style in which you do this counts; it is a reflection of who you are. Your style sets the tone not just for a pretty table, but for so much more.

Just as the year has a rhythm of seasons, so does a day; the atmosphere of a space will subtly change as both the day and the seasons unfold. The dining table plays a role that is central to the rhythm of a home. Where one day there are tears falling in a cup of coffee, in that same spot will be laughter on another occasion. Just as nature has seasons and moods, so too do we. And my kitchen table has seen it all. What laughter, tears, love, and just about every other emotion one could imagine, has fallen upon that table. We eat, celebrate holidays, entertain, do homework, cook, gossip, unpack groceries, linger over cups of coffee, paint, pay bills. It's polished with beeswax and scrubbed down with soap; covered one hour in sticky jam, the next in homework, and later still is glowing in candlelight ready for an evening meal. The duality of this space is fascinating; it is an immediate reflection of the range of emotions and moods that a home harbors. In turn the physical space needs to be fluid, flexible, and open to spontaneity to happily accommodate this multiplicity of emotions.

One of the greatest inspirations for freshening your home is arriving home with an armload of groceries and flowers fresh from the market. There is something so fundamental about the weekly renewal of food supplies in the home, about feeding a family or sharing food with friends. It is an age-old ritual—not just a chore but a way of

Gathering and entertaining

A few bold gestures mark the season. A disused fireplace doubles as a stage set for seasonal vignettes. **far left** For winter it is filled with church candles surrounded by twigs collected on a weekend walk. The large bunch of mistletoe hangs above as a symbol of the season. The home-made chair covers are a pretty touch, contrasting nicely with the coolness of the room. **left** A summer landscape is layered with quick watercolor studies painted of the sky each weekend over the summer months. A toy boat from childhood stays in use as a memento of summers past. **below** African daisies in galvanized pots hanging on a blank wall bring nature closer to the window and enliven the view.

showing your love. The colors of the changing seasons bring life to the room. My kitchen table has become the place of honor where I routinely place a small still life of natural objects. It could be as plain as a mixing bowl filled with nectarines or a pitcher overflowing with wildflowers. Maybe it is only noticed at a glance, but hopefully it serves as a point for those who pass to stop, look, and if only briefly think "oh, how beautiful." It is a small gesture, but who knows the value of a moment's beauty? I look at it as a gift, a way of showing my love for my friends and family, and perhaps enriching their day by causing a brief pause in their busy lives to awe at a flash of nature's wonder.

Parties with a seasonal theme give a great excuse for more elaborate decoration. And you don't have to restrict yourself to the obvious celebrations, such as Christmas and Halloween. Different cultures have their own traditions. The Japanese have cherry blossom parties in the spring, when friends and family gather under the trees to watch the blossoms fall. Celebrate on a smaller scale by bringing a few stems of cherry blossom indoors and placing them in a pitcher on your kitchen table to force them into bloom. At the height of summer, celebrate the solstice as the Swedish do. Make daisy chains, have everyone wear white, freeze vodka, and serve it with fresh edible flowers such as bright orange and red nasturtiums with their peppery petals. In the fall hold a harvest festival dinner. To create a completely different informal dining atmosphere use a pallet or a low coffee table covered with a big cloth or kilim and surround it with all the pillows in the house for seating, Go over the top with candles by placing them on every appropriate surface, and let them serve as your only lighting, Serve pumpkin soup out of a hollowed-out pumpkin.

Changing your dining table can be achieved simply with the throw of a cloth and a centerpiece that reflects the season. Usually natural elements work the best. A dining table can be transformed for an event with the simple throw of a tablecloth. Different patterns and textures lend themselves to different times of year.

A small outside space becomes an informal eating area in summer. **top far left** The chandelier will be brought inside to warm the house in winter but here it gets an airing and provides a frame for pots of flowers. **bottom far left** A tumbler is filled to bursting with small sprigs and flower heads plucked from the garden. **left** Layers of textiles set a scene conducive to a long afternoon's relaxation. **above** The vibrant colors of the kilims and robust canvas cushion covers reflect the palette of the garden.

right and far right Textiles added or subtracted as the weather dictates make a distinctive change in the mood of this room. Even the smallest change such as the objects on this mantel incite a moment's contemplation and add to the stimulating feel of a house that is very much in motion. **above** An artful juxtoposition of textures and shapes makes for intriguing still lifes. **far right below** A summer story of whites is made up of such incongruous items as a candle, a pitcher of flowers from the yard, and a necklace.

For instance, gingham always looks fresh in the spring-time alongside a jar of daffodils. Layering cloths can take a textile from one season into another. A pretty white embroidered tablecloth looks light and airy in summer but can be layered over something more textural such as a rough linen sheet when cooler weather calls for something more substantial. Dining chairs can be a group of mismatched secondhand market finds, perhaps all painted one color for unity. Even the humblest dining chair can look elegant when it is dressed up in a home-made slipcover.

Dreaming and refreshing

THE BEDROOM IS OUR MOST PERSONAL SPACE. IT CONTAINS OUR MOST INTIMATE THOUGHTS AND POSSESSIONS AND STAYS VEILED FROM THE VIEW OF THE OUTSIDE WORLD. IT IS A HAVEN WITHIN THE HAVEN OF HOME, THE SAFEST PLACE WITHIN A SAFE PLACE. A BEDROOM IS WHERE OUR DREAMS AND IMAGINATIONS CAN FEEL SECURE ENOUGH TO FLOAT AS FAR AS THEY CAN GO. Creativity is without boundaries and our thoughts can have full sway. It should be a room that harbors intimacy, allowing you to truly be yourself. It is a place to retreat to, where you can rejuvenate; a place to be alone with your thoughts. More than any other activity the patterns of sleep are linked into nature's cycle. The changing lengths of day and nights affect our circadian rhythms, so that in the depths of winter we struggle from sleep when the alarm wakes us, but in summer, sunlight awakens us more gently. The intimacy of a bedroom allows for a certain vulnerability. It is said that chidren's minds are most open just before they fall asleep. Have you ever stayed awake in the darkness with a child, friend, or lover just talking? Somehow the security of a bedroom and the blanket of darkness allows for this type of openness, where the barriers we put up around us to face the outside world can be taken down, allowing our minds to just drift.

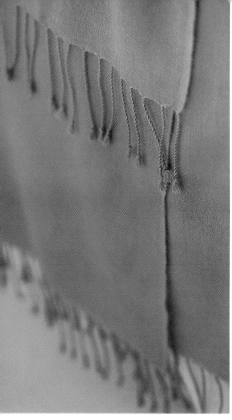

Layers of cashmere throws and pillows in a variety of colors become a vehicle to adapt the mood of a bed from one season to the next. **above** Sherbet colors suggest summer fruits and berries. **right** Mosquito netting transforms an otherwise functional sleeping area into a romantic summer retreat. **far right** A layer of basic white bedlinen is versatile enough to carry different looks throughout the year. **top far right** Soft cashmere pajamas offer the ultimate in winter comfort and luxuriance. **bottom far right** Bedside posies pick up the changing colors.

The bedroom is where your whole mind and body come into repose. To make an atmosphere that is conducive to this feeling, surround yourself only with things that make you feel good. This is the place where you can really indulge your senses with tactile fabrics, soothing scents, harmonious colors, and soulful music. The proper lighting is essential to the mood, and a dimmer switch is a great idea in the bedroom as it can easily change the space from a practical one where you apply your make-up to a romantic or restful one. Satisfy your physical need to be comforted. In winter when the weather is dull a huge knitted bed throw of the softest yarn and an amaryllis blooming on the radiator may be all that is needed to chase the winter blues away. In summer a cool breezy atmosphere with simple white bed linen and the scent of lavender drifting in from an open window can be a welcome relief after a long, hot day.

Working as a fashion designer, I use fabric and accessories in a seasonal way. I love the anticipation of each coming season, changing my wardrobe from winter woolens to spring cottons and summer linens. Therefore it was only natural for me to approach my home in a seasonal manner also. I realized my rooms should change like my wardrobe did. And just as in my wardrobe I have my basics, I have

them for my home also. Year round, fine white bedding works as a base for a soothing restful look. Onto this, layer textures and patterns as your mood dictates. Gone are the days when we thought we had to have a matching set of sheets. Pile layers on as the weather gets colder and peel them off as the warm weather arrives. Think of it as putting together a wardrobe for your bed.

The simplest way to change the feel of a bedroom is by changing the bed linen. A fresh duvet cover especially can change the entire look of the room in one bold stroke. Unfortunately, really attractive ones are hard to track down and they can be unbelievably expensive.

When decorating with an all-white palette, texture plays an important role in reflecting the changing seasons. **far left** Space is one of the biggest luxuries we have today. The all-white palette and sparse furnishings of this room exaggerate the space, lending the room a calm and peaceful feeling. **center left** Functional metal mugs and a florist's bucket used as vases lend a certain no-nonsense approach to decorating. In contrast to this the flower sprigs add softness and a heavenly

aroma to the room. **center right** The clean mimimal atmosphere of the room remains constant through the year, but in readiness for cooler weather there are piles of throws and bed covers. Enormous pillows will be propped up at the end of the bed for comfortable nighttime reading. **above** A play of textures—juxtaposing the luxury of a cashmere throw and mohair blanket against the sparseness of the room makes for a sensuous mix of hard against soft.

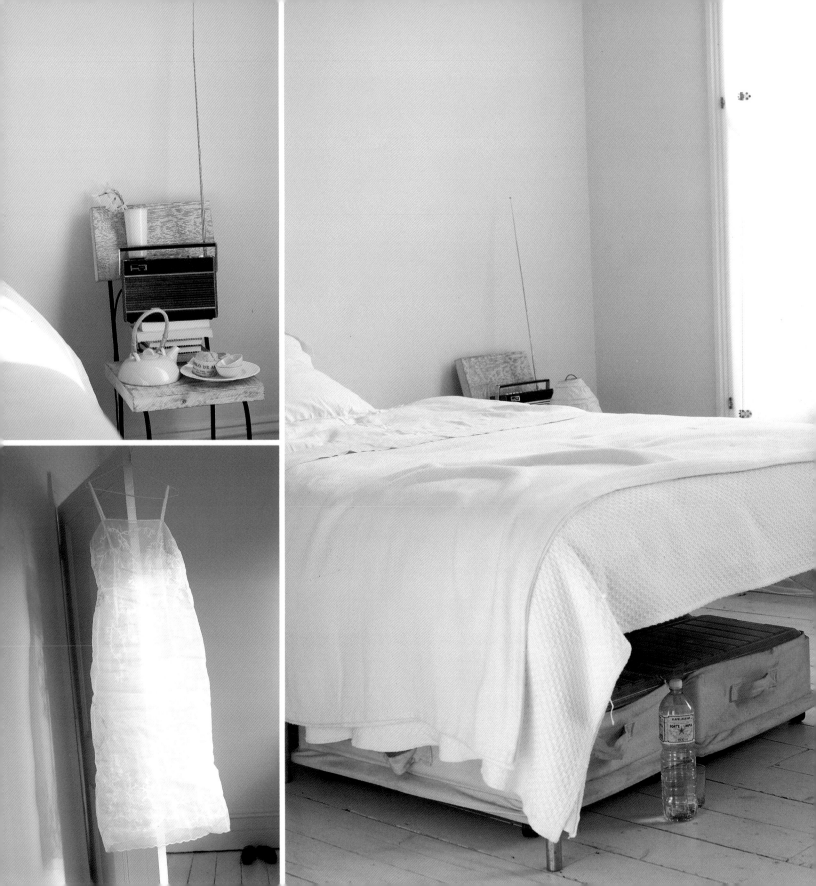

top far left The smallest touch can hint at a season. A bedside posy of a few narcissus buds is replaced by a favorite postcard, evoking an earthy feel in the winter months. **bottom far left** A dress caught momentarily hanging from the door becomes a temporary still life, a play of light and shadow. **left** Thin pure cotton bed covers are light and easy in summer. **below** A fur throw maintains the look without sacrificing comfort.

Try making your own covers by sewing two sheets together, perhaps adding a linen flange around the edge such as you would find on a pillowcase. Or try making one in a patchwork of leftover fabrics. Likewise, inexpensive simple white cotton sheets and pillowcases can be personalized with trimmings such as adding piqué borders at the edges, or a pretty ribbon running along the top—even some antique buttons added as a closure on a pillowcase can give a special twist. Work with contrasts: if you decide you want a romantic bed with piles of white lace ruffles, complement this by keeping the rest of the room bare for drama.

Look to your wardrobe, not only to find the key to your style, but as a source of

Create wardrobes for your bed that evolve from season to season

accessories for your home. A collection of bead necklaces need not be relegated to a jewelry box, but can be put on display hanging from a door knob, or even used as tie-backs for drapes. Similarly, a beautiful scarf or shawl can be displayed simply hanging from a nail in the wall. Group your jewelry and accessories neatly in a row of shallow baskets and place them on a bench against one wall for easy access. You can get as much pleasure from displaying favorite items from your wardrobe and looking at them every day as you do from wearing them. Resist the temptation to go out and buy new things for your home, when there is a whole box of goodies tucked away in your closet.

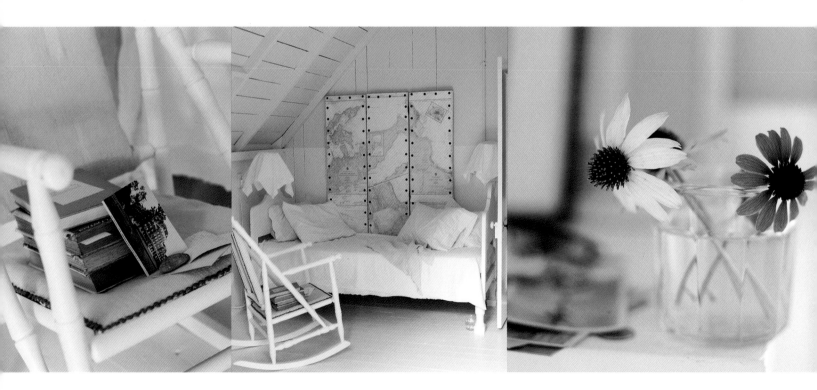

Walking into this bedroom feels like going on vacation. **below, from left** A mixture of thrift-shop furniture has all been painted white for a more cohesive look. The palest aqua hints at summer skies. Casual touches such as shirts hanging from pegs on the wall reflect the laid-back lifestyle of summer. **right** Small incidental flowers are as effective as large displays and lend themselves to the effortless air of this summer room.

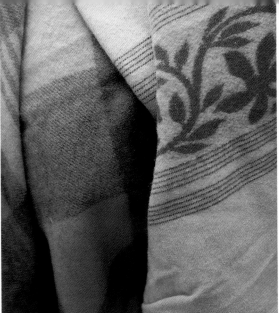

One of my most cherished moments of the day is the earliest hours of the morning when my husband and I are woken by the sound of small feet making their way into our bedroom. Our two young boys sleepily climb into bed with us and we all start the day slowly waking up together. Sometimes we just sit in silence together, sometimes there are giggles, and coffee cups have been known to topple onto the bed. For me it is the most cherished moment of day. I love the thought that, without fail, every morning the bed my husband and I share becomes a family bed. Those few moments work as a point of contact for us as a family before we all

The Scandinavian feel of this room sits just as well in hot and cold weather. The cool blue colors evoke a winter's landscape and easily become a seaside memory in summer. **left** Paper snowflake cutouts echo the gently falling snow outside. **above, from left** The first glimpse of a simple pose of a few objects from the doorway of a room sets the tone for what is around the corner. Vintage blankets have wonderfully colors that have mellowed

from years of frequent washing. The bed is piled with warm woolly blankets and plenty of pillows to snuggle into on a winters night. **below, from left** The cushion covers are handmade with easy linen ties for closure. In the summer months seaside stripes in cotton come out of storage to replace the winter woolens, turning this bedroom into a cool and tempting retreat. Woven rope shoes easily make the move from the beach indoors.

venture out into the world. It is at moments like these in the intimacy of our bed that I truly feel the value of the sense of security and shelter that our home brings to us.

Small gestures that are meaningful to you are what make your house a home. Bedside tables tell the story of what is currently going on in your life. Fill it with a selection of books to lose yourself in, a scented candle, and a favorite postcard or photo. Small indulgent touches such as flowers by your bedside can make you feel especially pampered—I suppose it is the thought that they are there for only you to enjoy that makes them feel so luxurious.

Years ago my husband gave me a watercolor sketchbook in which he had painted a series of land- and skyscapes. I keep it on the mantelpiece next to my mirror in my bedroom and change the page according to the season and my mood. In summer my favorite page is a light and airy painting of clouds; in winter I tend to turn the page to one of the more earthy landscapes he painted of the plowed red fields of England. Not only is it a treasured gift, something that I love to look at every morning, but it also works as a reminder of the changing landscapes outside. It works as a personal touchstone for me, as this is a place I come to at least once in my daily routine.

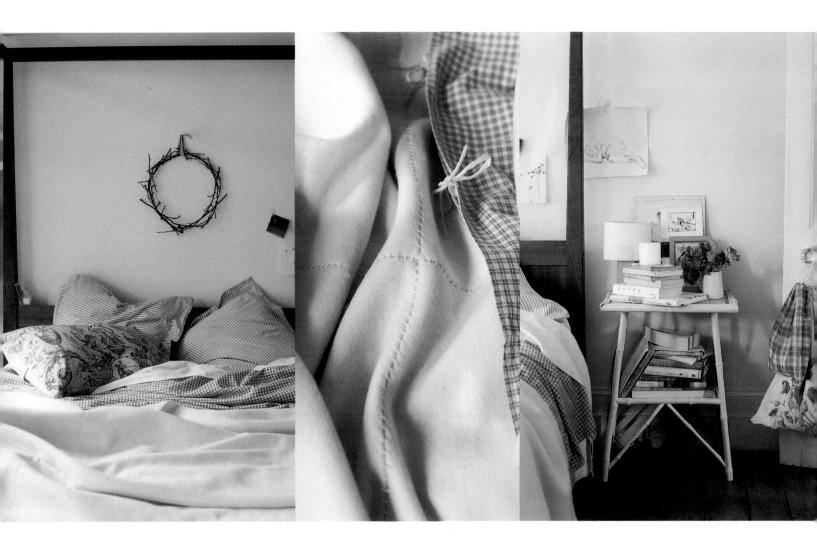

Bathrooms should be viewed just as indulgently as bedrooms, for they are equally personal spaces. We rarely think to place flowers here, but just a few sprays of eucalyptus or one or two sweet peas in a tooth mug next to the basin will give a lift to your spirits first thing in the morning and last thing at night when you brush your teeth, and the steamy atmosphere will bring out their scent. Bathrooms naturally lend themselves to a summery treatment, perhaps because the associations with water suggest a blue or green color treatment. But they can be transformed into winter havens with an abundance of thick fleecy towels and generous amounts of candlelight.

Borrowing from fashion adds a playful sense of surprise in this bedroom throughout the year. **above, from left** Vintage handkerchiefs are stitched onto brightly colored throw pillows. The white pillowcases are made from plain white sheeting, with grandma's old lace cocktail napkins appliquéd on the front. A jar is used temporarily as a vase, filled with geraniums that make economical and lasting cut flowers. A love note pressed between glass with rose petals stays by the bedside table. A wreath fashioned from branches collected in an apple orchard is a token of winter and the completion of the year. A slightly irreverent mix of pattern keeps the room from becoming too serious. A warm blanket was made by stitching together large squares of cream wool. The bedside table gets cluttered with winter's activities and interests: sketches are taped casually on the wall to allow for an easy change of scenery. Drawstring bags are made from vintage clothing.

Sometimes a room stays in one season all year; the double aspect of this small bathroom ensures that it is flooded with light all year round. Light linen café curtains allow for privacy without hindering the light streaming in or the view. The shower curtain is fashioned from a sheer embroidered cotton lined with plastic and adorned with old curtain clips found in a second-hand market. **right** A space is transformed with candlelight, making a winter's bath a soul-sustaining ritual. Pampering is a much-needed escape when the weather turns harsh.

Source directory

The publisher and the author of *A Home For All Seasons* are not responsible for the products sold by the following companies, and it is not our intention to promote any of these purveyors.

Furniture and accessories

ABC Carpet & Home
881–888 Broadway
New York
NY10003
212-674-1144
www.abc.home
Home furnishings, fabrics, carpets and design accessories

Bed, Bath & Beyond
620 Avenue of the Americas
New York
NY 10011
212-255-3550
www.bedbathand
   beyond.com
Everything for the bedroom and bathroom, plus home decor and much more

Ruby Beets Antiques
Poxybogue Road
Bridgehampton
New York
NY 11932
516-537-2802
Antique painted furniture, old china, and kitchenware

Bloomingdales
1000 Third Avenue
New York
NY 10022
212-705-2000
www.bloomingdales.com
Beloved department store, for classic furnishings

Crate & Barrel
646 N Michigan Avenue
Chicago
IL 60611
800-996-9960
www.crateandbarrel.com
A one-stop store for good-value furniture and accessories

Hold Everything
1309–1311 Second Avenue
New York
NY 10021
212-879-1450
www.williamssonoma.com
   /brands/brands.clm
Storage, accessories, and furniture of all kinds

Ikea
1800 East Mc Connor Parkway
Scaumburg
IL 60173
www.ikea.com
Scandinavian furniture and great accessories for the home

Jennifer Convertibles
3302/3304 M Street NW
Washington
DC 20007
202-333-0080
www.jenniferfurniture.com
Full selection of sleeper sofas, rugs, and sheets for any decor

Portico Bed & Bath
139 Spring Street
New York
NY 10012
212-941-7800
Elegant bed linen and bath accessories

Pottery Barn
600 Broadway
New York
NY 10012
800-922-5507
www.potterybarn.com
Accessories for the home and garden

Restoration Hardware
935 Broadway
New York
NY 10011
212-260-9479
www.restorationhardware
   .com
Not just hardware, but reproduction furnishings, knicknacks for the home and garden

Williams-Sonoma
121 East 59th Street
New York
NY 10022
800-541-1262
www.williams-sonoma.com
Great kitchenware

Fabrics and trimmings

Birtex Fabrics
146 Geary Street
San Francisco
CA 94108
415-392-2910
www.birtexfabrics.com
Wide variety of ribbons, trims, and notions

Calico Fabric Shop
52 Main Street
Florence
MA 01062
413-585-8665
www.calicofabric.com
Over 3,000 bolts of fabrics,
featuring a helpful and
informative staff

Hyman Hendler & Sons
67 West 38th Street
New York
NY 10018
212-840-8393
www.hymanhendler.com
Fabulous selection of
ribbons

The Ribbonerie Inc.
191 Potrero Avenue
San Francisco
CA 94103
415-626-6184
www.theribbonerie.com
Extensive collection of
ribbon

Rose Brand Textile Fabrics
517 West 35th Street
New York
NY 10001
212-594-7424
Theatrical trade suppliers; a
good source for extra-wide
fabrics, including muslin,
canvas, scrim, and ticking

Vicotoria Louise, Mercers
P.O. Box 266
Jefferson
MD 21755
301-473-4949
www.fred.net/stull/
    victoria.html
Fine ribbons, laces, and
historical materials

Garden accessories
and plants

Adkins Architectural
Antique
3515 Fannin Street
Houston
TX 77004
800-522-6547
www.adkinsantiques.com
Salvage architectural
artifacts, including urns
and gargoyles

Anthropologie
375 West Broadway
New York
NY 10012
800-309-2500
www.anthropologie.com
Good selection of garden
accessories with lots of
interesting pots

The Home Depot
2455 Paces Ferry Road
Atlanta
GA 30339
800-430-3376
www.homedepot.com
Chainstore with home and
garden supplies

Van Bourgondien Bros.
P.O. Box 100
Babylon
BY 11702–9004
800-622-9997
Bulbs, including dwarf
oriental lilies

Paint

The Art Store
600 Martin Luther King Jr.
Parkway
Des Moines
Iowa 50312
515-244-7000 or
800-652-2225
Speciality decoratiing shop
for brushes, enamels, paints,
varnish, and powders

Janovic
1150 Third Avenue
New York
NY 10021
800-772-4381
www.janovic.com
A quality selection of paints
in a wide color range

Martha Stewart Paint
Collection
At Kmart
888-627-8429
Online store locator:
www.bluelight.com
Selection of decorator
shades

Pearl Paint
3756 Roswell Road
Atlanta
GA 30342
404-233-9400
www.pearlpaint.com
Wide variety of papers and
boards, plus fabric paints

Ralph Lauren Paint
Collection
At Ralph Lauren
867 Madison Avenue
New York
NY 10021
212-606-2100
800-379-7656 for stockists
A vast collection of
wonderful colors

Acknowledgments

Thanks to the following people for their help
with this book:

Victoria Bailey for her creative spirit
Angela Miller for her endless support
Lisa Hoss Panitz for her enthusiam
Sian Parkhouse for her dedication
Jacqui Small for her vision
James Merrell for his eye

Thanks to everyone at Ryland Peters & Small.

A big thanks to everyone who so graciously opened their
homes to be photographed for this book and who each in
turn was an inspiration: Ann Shore, K. Russell Glover and
Angela Miller, Tom Fallon, Sig Bergamin, Gabriele Sanders,
Katsuji Asada, Janet and Hiroshi Kazo, Janie Jackson, Barbara
Davis and her family, Liz Dougherty Pierce.

But especially to Dave, Josh, and Ben for . . . well, just about
everything.

The publishers would like to acknowledge the work of Janie Jackson,
stylist/designer, whose work appears on the front cover and on page 94 top
right, pages 86–87, and pages 114–17, and the work of William and Barbara
Davis, designer, New York State (telephone 607-264-3673), whose work
appears on page 4 center, page 34 left and bottom left, page 41 upper right
and lower right, page 78, page 100, and pages 120–21.